Castles

Stephanie Turnbull

Designed by Laura Parker

Illustrated by Colin King

Cover illustration by Ian Jackson

Additional illustrations by Adam Larkum

Castle consultant: Abigail Wheatley, PhD,
Centre for Medieval Studies, University of York

Reading consultant: Alison Kelly,
Roehampton University

Contents

High on a hill

The ruins of a huge stone castle stand on a hill. Hundreds of years ago, this castle was full of people.

Some castles were built on cliffs, so they had a good view out to sea.

A huge home

Castles were built for rich people such as lords and ladies or kings and queens.

Servants worked and lived in the castle grounds.

Soldiers guarded the castle gate.

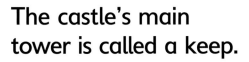

The castle's main
tower is called a keep.

A thick wall was
built to keep
enemies out.

Rich people had two or three castles. If they
were tired of one, they moved to another.

Types of castles

Some castles were made of wood. The keep was built on a high mound of earth.

Keep

Other castles were made of stone. They had strong towers and thick walls.

Building a castle sometimes took more than 20 years.

Some castles had water around them.
This is called a moat. The moat helped
to keep out enemies.

People crossed the
moat on a wooden
platform called
a drawbridge.

The drawbridge
was pulled up with
chains if an enemy
came near.

The keep

There were lots of rooms inside the keep.
The best rooms belonged to the lord and his family.

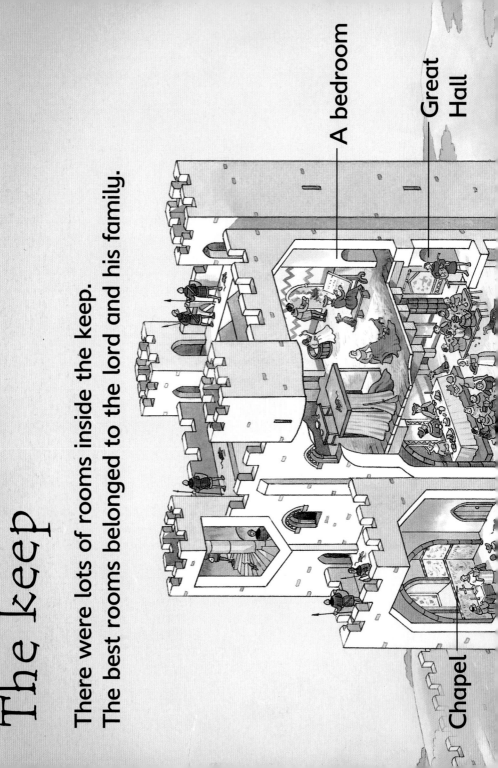

A bedroom

Great
Hall

Chapel

Guard room

Storeroom

A castle toilet was just a hole in the floor. Underneath was a chute that led to a pit outside.

Castles were always full of rats. Can you spot ten rats in the keep?

9

Castle life

Castle owners lived in comfortable rooms.
They slept in big, soft beds like this red one.

Curtains around
the bed kept them
snug and warm.

Servants had to
sleep on the
hard, cold floor.

People in castles got up early. Sometimes
a bell was rung at dawn to wake everyone.

Stone castles could be damp and chilly.
Huge fires helped to keep rooms warm.

People had baths in big wooden tubs.
Servants heated the water over a fire.

Castles were noisy places. Servants worked,
children played games and dogs barked.

Fun and games

There were no televisions in castle times. People had to find other things to do.

Acrobats often visited castles to put on shows.

Jugglers juggled balls or knives.

Musicians sang songs and played instruments.

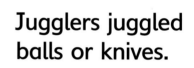

Many castles had a jester. His job was to tell jokes and make everyone laugh.

This picture was painted about 700 years ago. It shows a group of musicians playing tunes for a king.

Hunting

Lords and ladies enjoyed hunting.
Birds called falcons were trained to hunt.
Here are four stages of training a falcon.

1. The falcon got used to being carried and fed.

2. It was kept on a rope, and flew after bits of food.

3. Later, the falcon was able to fly freely.

4. It killed small birds and came back to its owner.

A hood helped to keep the falcon calm when it was taken out to be trained.

It was very fashionable to own a falcon. People took them everywhere.

In the kitchen

The kitchen was a building in the castle grounds. All the meals were made there.

Meat was roasted over a fire, on a stick called a spit.

This is how part of a castle kitchen might have looked.

1. To bake bread, bakers lit a fire in an oven to heat it up.

2. They mixed dough for bread and made it into loaves.

3. The loaves went in the oven when the fire died down.

4. The oven was still hot, so the bread soon cooked.

Castles didn't have refrigerators, so food went bad quickly. Cooks added spices to disguise the horrible taste.

Fabulous feasts

Huge meals called feasts were served in the Great Hall of the castle.

Important guests sat at a high table.

Everyone else sat on long benches.

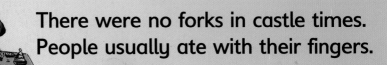

There were no forks in castle times. People usually ate with their fingers.

People ate lots
of meat and fish.

Cooks decorated food
with feathers and fruit.

Amazing models made of sugar and paper
were carried in to impress the guests.

Knights

Knights were rich, important soldiers. They helped to protect castles against enemies.

Knights had shapes or pictures on their shields. Each knight had his own pattern.

First a
knight put
on a thick,
padded vest.

Over this
he wore a
shirt made
of metal.

Metal plates
covered his
arms, legs
and chest.

Then he put
on a long
top and
big gloves.

He wore a
heavy metal
helmet on
his head.

He carried
a wooden
shield to
protect him.

At a joust

A joust was a pretend fight between two knights.

The knights held long poles called lances.

They rode on strong horses called chargers.

The winner of a joust got a prize. Sometimes he won the losing knight's horse and weapons.

The two knights charged up to each other,
on a narrow track.

Each knight tried to push the other one off
his horse with a lance.

The knight who was able to stay on his
horse was the winner.

Attack!

Sometimes castles were attacked. Enemies often used a machine called a catapult.

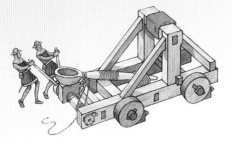

1. Soldiers pulled a big lever back.

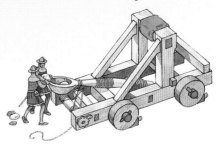

2. They loaded it with heavy rocks.

3. Then they let the lever spring up.

4. The rocks hit the castle walls.

Enemies often catapulted dead animals into castles, to spread diseases.

This old painting shows a huge battle in front of a castle as enemies try to take it over.

Fighting back

Soldiers tried to keep their castle safe from enemies.

They dropped rocks or boiling water onto the heads of enemies who came near.

Sometimes enemies tried to sneak into castles in disguise.

The soldiers were armed with bows and sharp arrows.

They fired arrows through thin slits in the wall.

This castle has many arrow slits in its walls. Soldiers also shot arrows from the roof.

Castles in ruins

Most castles are now empty. They have crumbled over the years.

This is how Raglan Castle, in Wales, might have looked 400 years ago.

This is how the castle looks now.

Some castles
were destroyed
by enemies
in attacks.

This tower
was blown up,
but part of it
still stands.

A few castles have been
rebuilt for people to live in.

Glossary of castle words

Here are some of the words in this book you might not know. This page tells you what they mean.

 keep - the main tower of a castle. It usually had a wall around it.

 drawbridge - a bridge that was pulled up to keep enemies out of a castle.

 falcon - a type of large bird. Falcons can be trained to hunt smaller birds.

 feast - a huge meal for lots of people, with plenty to eat and drink.

 shield - a tough, wooden plate. Knights used shields to protect themselves.

 joust - a game where two knights tried to knock each other off their horses.

 catapult - a machine that could fling rocks and other things through the air.

Websites to visit

You can visit exciting websites to find out more about castles.

To visit these websites, go to the Usborne Quicklinks Website at **www.usborne-quicklinks.com** Read the internet safety guidelines, and then type the keywords "**beginners castles**".

The websites are regularly reviewed and the links in Usborne Quicklinks are updated. However, Usborne Publishing is not responsible, and does not accept liability, for the content or availability of any website other than its own. We recommend that children are supervised while on the internet.

Neuschwanstein Castle was built for a German king, but he died before it was finished.

Index

Acknowledgements

Photographic manipulation by Emma Julings
With thanks to Grace Bryan-Brown and The National Trust for the model on page 19.

Photo credits

The publishers are grateful to the following for permission to reproduce material:
© **The Bridgeman Art Library:** 1 (Bibliotheque Royale de Belgique, Brussels, Belgium); © **Corbis:** 2-3 Dunnottar Castle (Charles Philip), 15 (Yann Arthus-Bertrand), 25 (Historical Picture Archive), 27 (Araldo de Luca), 28 (Chris Bland; Eye Ubiquitous), 31 Neuschwanstein Castle (Ric Ergenbright); **Crown Copyright CADW: Welsh Historic Monuments:** 20; © **E & E Picture Library:** 7 Bodiam Castle (Mike Morton); © **English Heritage Photo Library:** 29 Helmsley Castle; © **Getty Images:** 6 Alcazar Castle (Gary Cralle), 22 (Pete Dancs); **Crown copyright: Historic Royal Palaces:** 16 (detail of the Great Kitchen, Hampton Court Palace); © **Lebrecht Collection:** 13; © **Leeds Castle:** 10 (Angelo Hornak).

Every effort has been made to trace and acknowledge ownership of copyright. If any rights have been omitted, the publishers offer to rectify this in any subsequent editions following notification.